T0156904

Business Laws
PR*from*VERBS

DAVID**LOCKWOOD**

WESTBOW*
PRESS
A DIVISION OF THOMAS NELSON
& ZONDERVAN

Scripture taken from *Holy Bible* King James Version

Cover Design | Danielle Zackarias

WestBow Press books may be ordered through booksellers or by contacting:

WestBow Press
A Division of Thomas Nelson & Zondervan
1663 Liberty Drive
Bloomington, IN 47403
www.westbowpress.com
1 (866) 928-1240

ISBN: 978-1-4908-7796-9 (sc)
ISBN: 978-1-4908-7797-6 (hc)
ISBN: 978-1-4908-7795-2 (e)

Library of Congress Control Number: 2015906622

Print information available on the last page.

WestBow Press rev. date: 05/07/2015

Contents

To Donald and Kathleen Miller—true examples
of life, light, courage, and faith.

Introduction

You are in business. Whether you are a student, parent, public servant, production worker, member of clergy, or an entrepreneur, you are in the business of producing a lifestyle of quality and excellence. Your progress in life requires personal growth and organizational development, which are the results of applying the laws of business found in Proverbs.

Reading Proverbs is part of my daily discipline and routine study, and it has become one of the most important aspects of my personal achievement, which is why I wrote *Business Laws from Proverbs*. I want to share with you how the laws are working for me and for others, and how they can also work for you.

Each of the thirty-one sections of this devotional explains a law I have gleaned from a chapter in Proverbs and how I have experienced that law. My hope is that you will be inspired to apply each law, because I want to add value to your day and life, as value has been added to mine.

Each day, read in your Bible the suggested chapter in Proverbs and reflect on the law and explanations. Make notes as God inspires you, and look for ways to connect the principles through application to your daily endeavors.

In this book I reference leaders because we are all leaders no matter our status. Leadership is influence, and each of us influences others. These thirty-one business laws can positively influence the value we add to other people.

The goal is to live successfully. God wants us to be fulfilled in every area of our lives. As our wisdom and understanding increase, so will our levels of achievement and reward.

1

Law of Association

Read Proverbs 1. Reflect on verse 5.

> A wise man will hear, and will increase
> learning; and a man of understanding shall
> attain unto wise counsels.

Successful people know who to associate with, who to listen to, and whose advice to follow. A business partner once told me, "It's as much who knows you as who you know that determines outcome."

My partner was referring to the power of affiliation, and the principle applies universally. We assimilate the characters and attributes of those we spend time with. A Spanish proverb states, "Tell me who you run with, and I'll tell you who you are."

Perhaps as important, successful individuals are those who know who *not* to run with. They know whose advice *not* to follow. The proverb for today warns us of the dangers of negative association and rejecting wise counsel. It ends by stating that those who listen to divine prompting will dwell safely and be quiet from fear of evil. I want to live protected from terror and turmoil. Don't we all? Especially when the news media reminds us of violence often too close to our borders.

These days we hear myriad voices. Technology has made information more available than ever. But all information is not helpful, and all advice is not beneficial. How do we discern and filter the noise to obtain the wisdom we need?

First, we ask God to help us determine our personal identity, our purpose, and our direction in life. This process requires time and effort. Then we seek positive guides. We ask God to place people in our lives who will help us to reach our goals. We seek qualified leaders, teachers, and friends. We ask experts in our areas of interest for insight and perspective, and find and invest in good mentors. We obtain media resources on subjects we should learn about. And we read biographies of past and present icons successful in the same or similar fields.

The law of association reminds us to focus on what we should be pursuing, the people we should be spending time with, and the voices we should be listening to. If we choose the right associations, we will not have time in our schedules for associations that are not constructive. As believers, we can be alert to the voice of the Holy Spirit as He leads and guides us.[1]

Prayer

Heavenly Father,

Thank You for showing me Your direction for my life, family, finances, career, business, and legacy. Holy Spirit, fill my heart with Your counsel and understanding, so I may wisely apply the law of association.

Notes

_____

_____

_____

_____

_____

_____

_____

_____

I become like those whom I choose to be with.

—David R. Lockwood

2

Law of Seeking and Finding

Read Proverbs 2. Meditate on verses 4–5.

> If thou seekest her as silver, and searchest
> for her as for hid treasures; then shalt thou
> understand the fear of the LORD, and find the
> knowledge of God.

God enjoys a good treasure hunt. However, He perceives the reward as only half of the objective. The process that leads us to the reward is equally important. It is the phase in which we gain skill through exploration and active pursuit.

Wisdom is often not easy to find. It requires diligent searching in nonobvious places. One way I seek wisdom is through the habit of reading a passage of Scripture each day. Proverbs is a good place to begin. As I read the passage and discover gems of wisdom, I gain an understanding of God's character. I learn that He protects us from harm.[1]

He keeps us on track, so we don't lose time in unproductive or meaningless tasks.[2] We come to know what pleases Him and how to solve problems in ways that are a win-win-win for God, others, and ourselves.[3] Our wealth is preserved through discretion, and we are preserved through divine understanding.[4]

We can apply the law of seeking and finding by simply asking for God's direction. Sometimes He speaks to us through reading biographies, attending conferences, or by getting together with people to exchange thoughts or creative ideas. In all our daily activities, we can ask the Holy Spirit to help us find the wisdom hidden within every moment.

In my early twenties, when I first opened my automotive sales and service business, I decided I wanted to know what other local entrepreneurs had done to be successful and how I might apply their experience to my situation. I didn't mind that they were from other industries, because I understood that the principles transferred regardless of market sector. I wanted to seek and find, as well as encourage them to do business with me. It was not uncommon for me to invite them to lunch. I asked questions. I placed my pride on my lap under the table, along with my napkin, and sought from them as much treasure in the form of knowledge as was polite.

Through the years, God has continued to bring individuals across my path. It has always been up to me to apply the law of seeking and finding to grow from the wisdom they share.

Prayer

Heavenly Father,

Thank You for helping me make seeking wisdom a daily habit. Thank You for teaching me the process I need to achieve the destiny You have placed within me. Thank You for the benefits Your wisdom allows me to enjoy when applying the law of seeking and finding.

Notes

_____

_____

_____

_____

_____

_____

_____

_____

God is never beyond the reach of our faith.

—David R. Lockwood

3

Law of Divine Partnership

Read Proverbs 3. Reflect on verses 5–6.

Trust in the LORD with all thine heart; and
lean not unto thine own understanding. In all
thy ways acknowledge him, and he shall direct
thy paths.

The principle that has most affected my understanding and
achievement of success is divine partnership. The law of divine
partnership enlists cooperation, association, collaboration,
affiliation, and connection between an individual and
God. Businesses create partnerships. Marriages require
partnerships. Parenting supports partnerships. Communities
offer partnerships. While risk is always inherent in human
partnerships, it is not a factor when one partners with God.

God is the only lifelong partner we can share absolutely
every aspect of our lives with. No one else offers the same
level of access or transparency. God is not biased or self-
centered. He focuses on our success and does not manipulate
or defraud our being. Knowing He wants us to grow and

thrive forms the foundation for trust, relationship, and cooperation with Him.

The law of divine partnership operates in the following manner: I work diligently to seek my objectives and life goals with all my mental, emotional, and physical capacities. I study, prepare, and continually add to what I can offer others, both in my personal and professional endeavors.

I constantly strive to improve my skills and abilities. I do this daily; however, I don't exclusively trust in my own talent to cause me to succeed. I trust in God's favor and providence through my personal relationship with Him. I once heard a preacher express it like this: "Pray like everything is up to God, and work like everything is up to you."

Choosing whether to trust in the grace and enabling of God or in our own experiences and abilities is a decision of the heart. That's why the passage says we are to trust in the Lord with all our heart and not depend on our own understanding. We are encouraged to seek knowledge, understanding, and wisdom. However, when times become challenging, or when we cannot see our way through, we need to trust and offer up all to God.

The grace and favor of God enables us to reach our goals. Partnering with God equips us to SEE | BE | DO | MORE. Applying the law of divine partnership requires us to have hearts of gratitude and trust, not hearts of pride and self-sufficiency.

Prayer

Heavenly Father,

I want to partner with You so I can be an excellent person for those whom I influence. Help me trust You and not lean to my own understanding. I want to apply the law of divine partnership and acknowledge You in all I do.

Notes

_____

_____

_____

_____

_____

_____

_____

_____

God is my senior partner. I hope to always remain a minority partner with Him.

—David R. Lockwood

4

Law of Growing

Read Proverbs 4. Reflect on verse 7.

> Wisdom is the principal thing; therefore get wisdom: and with all thy getting get understanding.

Wisdom invites us to grow. When we are young, growing seems to be something that just happens. As a child, I remember returning to the United States with my missionary family, and people who hadn't seen me for a while would greet me with, "My, how you've grown!" What was I to say? "Yeah, that's what happens when you're a kid. It's in the DNA."

It is God's natural design for us to grow and mature. However, as we get older, most of us don't want to be told, "My, how you've grown"—at least not literally. We would probably take it to mean our clothes appear larger. None of us want to be noticed in that way. Instead, we tell ourselves we're growing older. But are we truly growing, or are we slowly dying as we age?

I have lived in several places that attract retirees. I appreciate the time and insights they have shared. What puzzles me is that they often feel entitled to coast and settle for pleasure and rest. Growing is a season gone by. They seem to have forgotten that when we do not advance, we fall behind.[1]

When we stop growing, we begin dying. My mentor, John Maxwell, says some people die intellectually, emotionally, and sometimes even spiritually before dying physically.[2] Let this never be said of us!

Each day I apply the law of growing. I strive to grow spiritually by reading, meditating, speaking, and acting on God's Word. I grow intellectually and emotionally through studying, professional training, mentorship, and applying what I learn. I choose to improve my skills instead of escaping reality by watching another movie or television rerun.

I grow in physical health through a balanced diet and an active lifestyle. I eat the foods required to maintain good health. I choose to exercise. Otherwise what grows is not wisdom, but excess weight!

Parallel scenarios occur in business. When my staff and I do not sell products and services, we accumulate the weight of debt. We do not receive paychecks if we do not exercise and grow profit. The motivation to be compensated is a daily reminder to grow.

The law of growing reminds us that God designed within our DNA the ability to grow. We experience the consequences of demise when we choose not to.

Prayer

Heavenly Father,

Help me grow in knowledge, understanding, and wisdom. I want to apply the law of growing to my physical, mental, and spiritual well-being. Help me to help others grow as well.

Notes

_____

_____

_____

_____

_____

_____

_____

_____

In life we either grow or die; progress or regress.
—David R. Lockwood

5

Law of Access

Read Proverbs 5. Reflect on verses 8–9.

Remove thy way far from her, and come not
nigh the door of her house: lest thou give thine
honor unto others, and thy years unto the cruel.

The law of access cautions us to evaluate who we allow to
have access to our lives. Of particular warning is the alluring
seductress. In Genesis, Joseph demonstrates the best choice
of action: run![1]

People we are involved with in our friendships,
partnerships, professional associations, mentorships, and
other close relationships expect access to our lives. How much
of ourselves do we share with them? When we evaluate a
relationship, we should ask, "Am I wise to share myself with
this person? Is this person entitled to the time, energy, and
resources I may offer? What degree of access is appropriate?"
I also remind myself to consider the value I receive from
interacting within specific environments and diverse groups.

The law of access prods me to ask additional questions: "Is this a relationship from which I can learn more about the goals I have established for my life? Is the person I am connecting with a giver or a taker, and in what areas?" Later on I may consider the quality of a connection, and if it is one in which both parties are being edified. Some relationships are established for the purpose of business partnering or networking. Others focus more on spiritual growth. All should remain within context.

One further element to consider is that nobody can be everything to everyone. None of us can give what we don't have to offer, and we can't acquire from others what is not theirs to share.

What I endeavor to do is to ask the Holy Spirit to guide me in properly identifying individuals who should be allowed access to my life. Sometimes social networks stretch my discernment; nonetheless, I set guardrails for myself. I remember that access is a valued gift that each of us can potentially offer another. Are the individuals with whom we share our gifts worthy of our offerings?

God has placed wealth within each of us. It is best not to expose treasures of our lives with people who will not value and appreciate them—lest we cast pearls before swine and be devastated by poor judgment.[2] Heeding the law of access helps us discern. It cautions us to be wise.

Prayer

Heavenly Father,

Keep me from wrong relationships. Help me apply the law of access to carefully select connections and partnerships. Give me discernment to properly evaluate the access I allow others, and to place healthy boundaries with the people I relate to.

Notes

_____

_____

_____

_____

_____

_____

_____

_____

A person who will not add value to my space
is not welcome within my space.

—David R. Lockwood

6

Law of Action

Read Proverbs 6. Reflect on verses 6–8.

> Go to the ant ... consider her ways, and be
> wise: Which having no guide, overseer, or
> ruler, provideth her meat in the summer, and
> gathereth her food in the harvest.

Faith means to believe in someone or something. Faith requires action. Believing without corresponding action is dead.[1] In other words, faith has no value if we fail to support it by applying the law of action. In my life and business, I know I truly believe the internal dialogue of my own personal values when I externalize it with focused action. Actions are word enforcers. They are the bond of our reputation, the assurance of our commitment to others, and the proof of our obedience to God.

Before I started my automotive sales and service business years ago, I deliberated and speculated. After sufficient consideration, I took action. I put together a business plan, acquired loans, retained investors, hired employees, and began sales. I can tell you that speculating and taking action are not the same.

Here is another personal example. More than once in my past I have talked about getting into shape. The talking was a reminder, but I only accomplished progress toward my goal when I got on the treadmill and started walking. Once I started, the results provided motivation to continue.

The ants take action. They also have a wise plan. Ants do not collect food during the winter, as it is the wrong strategy for that time of year. I try to do the same. I continually check to ensure that the strategies my employees and I implement parallel the goals of our team, environment, season, resources, and ultimately our objectives.

Unfortunately, some people take action toward their goals with deficient strategies and then become disillusioned when they don't experience the results they expected. No one wants to make that mistake. We need to place our confidence in God while constantly applying natural principles and balancing the supernatural with the practical. We put our faith into action by applying wise principles in family, business, and public service. We give God something to bless, and then expect Him to bless the work of our hands.[2] Idleness and dereliction have no place in our lives when we apply the law of action.

Prayer

Heavenly Father,

Help me to be diligent and not slothful. Help me apply the law of action by being wisely productive in my life, family, business, and Your kingdom. Give me wisdom in planning my day and my way. I trust You to direct the actions I take.

Notes

_____

_____

_____

_____

_____

_____

_____

_____

Champions are both dreamers and doers.

—David R. Lockwood

7

Law of Focus

Read Proverbs 7. Reflect on verses 24–25.

Hearken unto me now therefore, O ye children,
and attend to the words of my mouth. Let not
thine heart decline to her ways, go not astray
in her paths.

The young man is in the wrong place, at the wrong time, with
the wrong people, doing the wrong thing. My interest in this
text goes beyond avoiding seduction. What stands out here
is why the young man was where he was to begin with. The
fact that he was strolling the streets at night tells me this man
didn't have his heart or mind focused on his purpose or goals.[1]
Rather, he was wandering aimlessly.

The passage doesn't say he went looking for trouble. On
the contrary, it says she caught him. Why? Because he was
in the wrong place. Why? Because he wasn't focused on
where he should be, and on what he should be doing. For
the young man, the consequences were detrimental and life
altering.

Focus gives us predetermined boundaries and parameters within which to make wise decisions. If our focus is properly aligned, we can assess potential opportunities to determine not just if they are good opportunities, but also if they are ideal for us specifically. We focus on one element at a time, and while our peripheral vision may be broad, our focused vision is acute to accurately perceive our goal.

Beware! Gals are not all that allures. Gold and glory seduce as well. We see it daily in the news. I will be candid enough to suggest we each have slipped on one of these. Here is my confession. A few years back, I was distracted by a business model opportunity that I knew nothing about and that was unrelated to my life goals. I thought it would bring needed results. I was wrong. Fortunately, I only lost a year of financial progress because of poor judgment. I regained focus and got back to the work that I was familiar with and called to do.

One more comment particularly for those who think gals, gold, or glory will never seduce them: The good is many times the enemy of the best. Knowing, preserving, and defending the focus God has given each of us requires effort and discipline. This principle truth is remarkable when we think about it: If we focus on that which should enter our lives, then that which should exit our lives fades by default—and this in itself is a miracle, and a residual of the law of focus.

Prayer

Heavenly Father,

Help me focus on what You have asked me to do. Help me discern the bad from the good from the best. Help me apply the law of focus by being in the right place, at the right time, with the right people—doing the right thing.

Notes

_____

_____

_____

_____

_____

_____

_____

_____

It is difficult to drive a car forward looking through the rearview mirror. It is also difficult to drive our lives that way.

—David R. Lockwood

8

Law of Creating Favor

Read Proverbs 8. Reflect on verse 35.

> For whoso findeth me [wisdom] findeth life,
> and shall obtain favor of the Lord.

We receive favor from God when we acquire wisdom. God desires us to be wise and experience life fulfilled. He wants to bless us with abilities, resources, and increase.

God tells us that the benefits of finding wisdom are more valuable than silver or gold.[1] He reminds us that wisdom is worth more than rubies; more than riches, honor, or power.[2] Why? Because when we possess the wisdom to solve problems for others, we obtain favor with them, as we do with God. We experience the blessings of being wise, favored, and prosperous all at the same time!

Applying the law of creating favor means that we look for problems to solve. We are creative in helping others think outside their self-imposed limitations to overcome challenges and grow.

One area in which I have helped solve problems is that of music leadership. I have shared my wisdom and gifting in music at churches in several countries and have received much favor, which has frequently opened further opportunities for speaking, teaching, and consulting.

I am persuaded that problem-solving affords wealth. I believe that the world will forever be indebted to those who take the initiative to solve problems. The greater the problem solved, the greater the reward.

The law of creating favor suggests that we amplify our skill sets, that we seek wisdom to be able to solve problems. Wisdom is hidden. It is safeguarded from those who do not value it or wish to apply it. The promise of life and favor is to those who find and apply wisdom.

As a child, I remember that I wanted to know more than I knew. I asked lots of questions and was constantly exploring. I wanted to discover and create new things. Now I share this mind-set with others through coaching and mentoring.

The aura of childlike wonder cultivates a lifestyle of learning. As we seek knowledge and wisdom and apply what we learn to helping others, we receive the benefits of applying the law of creating favor. The greater the favor we possess, the greater the influence and increase we will have as God leads us to SEE | BE | DO | MORE.

Prayer

Heavenly Father,

Help me pursue Your wisdom and apply the law of creating favor. I want to be an excellent problem solver for the people in my sphere of influence. As Your wisdom increases in my life, may Your favor and prosperity increase also.

Notes

_____

_____

_____

_____

_____

_____

_____

_____

Favor chases down the problem solvers.

—David R. Lockwood

9

Law of Preparation

Read Proverbs 9. Reflect on verse 9.

> Give instruction to a wise man, and he will
> be yet wiser: teach a just man, and he will
> increase in learning.

God has a way of showing us the panorama. In this passage,
He personifies wisdom as a woman who prepares her house
and invites guests who seek understanding. Those who
accept her invitation are nourished at her table. The passage
also implies that each individual has a choice between
accepting the invitation to receive wisdom or defaulting to
the foes of folly.

Daily we choose. Within the fourth dimension of time,
God created the duration of day. The continual fortitude
we need is naturally—and spiritually—distributed within
increments of the present moment. "Give us this day, our
daily bread," Jesus taught us to pray.[1] The woman of wisdom
summons those of us seeking wisdom to partake of the bread
of knowledge daily.

Proverbs reminds us that each day we have a choice: We can choose to exercise the habits God wants us to develop to reach the goals He has placed within us, or we can choose to neglect the daily deeds that determine the outcomes of our future. Doing right is a daily and sometimes painful process, but the benefits of acting wisely extend beyond sacrifices endured. Even as I sit here writing, I can choose to either watch a TV show that will do me little good, or to invest my time reflecting on wisdom to apply and share. How I spend my day dictates the direction of my destiny.

We choose to apply the law of preparation, because we want to add value to our own lives so we can add value to others. We want to SEE | BE | DO | MORE. The Enemy operates by the principle of temporary pleasure at the expense of our future. God operates by the principle of temporary sacrifice for our long-term fulfillment. Wise choices bring satisfaction. What are we thinking when we sacrifice our futures on the altar of immediate gratification? Do we realize we are becoming destined as fools?

When I face my computer screen each day, I remind myself of the law of preparation. I ask myself, Do the sites I visit prepare me for the future I wish to live? Answers are not necessarily easy or simple, but here is a question for each of us: Does the time we spend in various activities summon the wisdom that God wants us to share with others? Daily we choose to apply the law of preparation.

Prayer

Heavenly Father,

Help me apply the law of preparation so I become the person You created me to be. Help me do today what will bring the greatest satisfaction, fulfillment, and reward tomorrow.

Notes

_____

_____

_____

_____

_____

_____

_____

_____

The deeper the roots, the better the fruit.

—David R. Lockwood

10

Law of the Blessing

Read Proverbs 10. Reflect on verse 22.

> The blessing of the Lord, it maketh rich, and
> he addeth no sorrow with it.

I answered the phone and the call was from a colleague I had worked with years ago. I had left to start a business, while he had stayed with the corporation. He invited me to coffee, and we met a few days later.

The man wasted no time. "David, I see things have gone well for you in business and in general since you left. I'm at the end of my potential in my current environment. I feel frustrated from the lack of results I'm seeing, and I'm ready for a change. What do you suggest?"

I mentioned God's voice and my decision to add value to people through coaching and professional development, in addition to sales and marketing training. I shared my vision for entrepreneurial endeavors and mission outreaches in Latin America.

"The day job wasn't me," I told him, "and it wasn't what God wanted for me. I knew on the inside what I had to do." I went on to describe how I followed inner promptings, and how I now feel freer and more fulfilled. I encouraged my friend to do likewise and follow his own inner promptings.

God tells us, "If ye be willing and obedient, ye shall eat the good of the land."[1] Being willing and obedient are precursors. The law of the blessing is exemplified when we choose to obey. We find ourselves blessed in the city, the country, or wherever we live. Our family, work, and investments are blessed. Our banking accounts are blessed. Our property and possessions are blessed. We are blessed in travel, both coming and going. Our enemies may approach us, but they leave defeated.

The law of the blessing involves almighty God backing us in all we do, causing us to bloom where we are planted. God sanctifies our lives and our families. Others respect and honor us. God multiplies our belongings and makes us fruitful, and He shows favor on our behalf. We achieve a position of success where we lend and do not borrow. We see ourselves as above our challenges and not beneath.

I have found that when I sense God directing me and choose to follow Him continually, His grace causes me to follow after what pleases Him.[2] When we surrender our lives to God, decide to put Him first, and have the courage to follow Him, we experience the law of the blessing.[3]

Prayer

Heavenly Father,

I thank You that I am Yours. My life—past, present, and future—belongs to You. I ask that the law of the blessing abide on everything that I am, and in everything that I do in obedience to You.

Notes

_____

_____

_____

_____

_____

_____

_____

_____

God's blessing doesn't end with us. It begins
with us, that it may flow to others.

—David R. Lockwood

11

Law of Spreading Good News

Read Proverbs 11. Reflect on verses 24–26.

> There is that scattereth, and yet increaseth;
> and there is that withholdeth more than is
> meet, but it tendeth to poverty. The liberal soul
> shall be made fat: and he that watereth shall
> be watered also himself. He that withholdeth
> corn, the people shall curse him: but blessing
> shall be upon the head of him that selleth it.

Techniques for effective sales are found amidst the wisdom
of Proverbs, and for those of us who work in sales directly,
closing the deal is the most critical aspect of the job. St. Paul
knew this. He elaborated on the process preceding the closing
when he wrote, "How then shall they call on him in whom
they have not believed? And how shall they believe in him of
whom they have not heard? And how shall they hear without
a preacher?"[1]

Salespeople are some of the best paid *preachers* in business.
The reason is stated in the law of spreading good news.

Salespeople who demonstrate greater value in products and services reap greater income in return. They are blessed because they demonstrate value and provide elements that benefit others.

In business, we know we must offer a product or service that is worthwhile, adds value, and enhances the quality of life of the consumer. Because what we promote is of value, we can sell with confidence and firm belief. And for those who think they have absolutely no trace of or desire toward salesmanship, it is in everyone.

Salesmanship is as simple as posting something on a social network page or recommending a product or service to a friend or relative. It's called relational selling. A proof of belief is promotion. Similarly, if we truly trust what God says, we will tell others about His message as well.

Christians have the ultimate offering for people in desperate need: the good news of Jesus Christ, the hope of salvation, and the promise of healing. Restoration, deliverance, prosperity, power to overcome, and high quality of life—both now and in the life to come—are all part of the law of spreading good news.

Scripture is true. God continues to remind us, "Behold, the righteous shall be recompensed in the earth."[2] I also tell myself, "I had fainted, unless I had believed to see the goodness of the LORD in the land of the living."[3] Each day God gives us much to share. May we never withhold His good news nor our own unique value from others.

Prayer

Heavenly Father,

I ask You to help me use my talents and abilities to apply law of spreading the good news. Help me share what You have given me, and find success in adding value to others.

Notes

_____

_____

_____

_____

_____

_____

_____

_____

Spread words that build people up, not tear them down. Be generous with encouragement, stingy with criticism.

—David R. Lockwood

12

Law of Alignment

Read Proverbs 12. Reflect on verse 5.

> The thoughts of the righteous are right: but the
> counsels of the wicked are deceit.

The word *alignment* signals modern meditation, something
like *finding your center* or *being at peace with yourself*. While such
teachings encapsulate good concepts, they often focus on
alignment only to self, and not to God's will. The difference
is big.

No life ultimately succeeds when it is not aligned to God's
will. The greater the disconnect between differing areas of
our lives, the less successful we are. The more aligned we are,
the more success we achieve.

There have been times when I was drawn away from
God as my center point of reference. I spent too much time
emulating others whom I thought represented what I wanted.
Later I came to realize that what they promoted was not what
God wanted for me.

Alignment is not a one-time thing. Take cars, for example. A person can bring in a vehicle to get it aligned. The next day, the person hits a pothole. He didn't plan on running his wheel into the hole. He could say it wasn't his fault—the road should have been in better condition. But it wasn't.

The alignment then has changed. After a few of these rough riding episodes, the driver should have his vehicle realigned. Even if a person never hits a hole in the road, wear on tires eventually results in the need for alignment.

The same holds for daily affairs. The wear of life continually invites us to realign ourselves with God. We often do this during church services, though spiritual alignment need not be reserved for sacred locations. God will meet us where we are. Our hearts are His concern, and from our hearts come true prayers. We can then align our thoughts, words, emotions, and actions to His will and ways. When we allow God to align us in these areas, we are better able to be in alignment with our families, finances, careers, and ministries of service.

When I allow the alignment of my spiritual life to steer too far one way or the other from my responsibilities in business and family, I suffer, as do my interactions with others. The law of alignment reminds me to keep my perspectives right with God.

Prayer

Heavenly Father,

Help me align my thoughts, words, and actions to Your will for me. I want to apply the law of alignment to that which I pursue. I want my relationships, education, business, and service to be in alignment with You.

Notes

_____

_____

_____

_____

_____

_____

_____

_____

Alignment with God will keep you from drifting on life's road.

—David R. Lockwood

13

Law of Right Speaking

Read Proverbs 13. Reflect on verses 2–3.

> A man shall eat good by the fruit of his mouth:
> but the soul of the transgressors shall eat
> violence. He that keepeth his mouth keepeth
> his life: but he that openeth wide his lips shall
> have destruction.

Words are powerful tools that shape our thoughts, focus, feelings, and futures. What we say today determines how we live tomorrow. Through the years, I have disciplined myself to speak positively about family, acquaintances, colleagues, business partners, and myself. I have also learned the value of restraining my words and remaining silent. Blessings beyond measure have been mine by applying of the law of right speaking.

If we believe the law of right speaking, we know that positive results come from declaring God's will and words over every aspect of our lives: mind, will, emotions, health, relationships, career, finances, and ministry. Growing up, I listened to a minister who used to say that words are seeds for a harvest. We choose the harvest we want.

I am reminded of an employee who one afternoon did what I never would have imagined. The damage he did to the car stirred much anger within me. The man who brought the car in for repair soon unleashed his anger on me. I listened. I applied the law of right speaking, and I continued to use wisdom when correcting my employee shortly thereafter.

What I had to do was take my frustration to God and ask Him to help me choose my words carefully. Years later, the employee returned. The honor he showed me affirmed that I had handled the challenge wisely. Instead of creating enemies, I righted wrongs and gained support through the event.

I might add that the law of right speaking seems to be one of the most difficult laws of wisdom to apply. St. James acknowledged this when he wrote that no man can tame the tongue.[1] We need the Holy Spirit to help us, and He will if we ask.

On the other hand, I frequently have the opportunity to provide positive, uplifting words to my employees, colleagues, and clients. The words we speak can change the spiritual and emotional climate of a room in minutes. The law of right speaking prompts us to consciously voice words that exhort and edify the lives of others.

Prayer

Heavenly Father,

Help me to speak the right words and refrain from speaking those that need not be voiced. I want to apply the law of right speaking. Help me be an encouragement to others, and to declare words of faith and hope to people in need.

Notes

_____

_____

_____

_____

_____

_____

_____

_____

The words, "Thank you," "I'm sorry," and "I love you," will never go out of style.

—David R. Lockwood

14

Law of Discernment

Read Proverbs 14. Reflect on verses 15–16.

> The simple believeth every word: but the
> prudent man looketh well to his going. A wise
> man feareth, and departeth from evil: but the
> fool rageth, and is confident.

Some people refer to discernment as a means of judging people and circumstances. Others speak of it as looking and thinking ahead. For me, discernment is the act of evaluation beyond the veneer of appearance.

Here is an example. I remember the time a man came to my office, stood across from my desk, and offered me a large volume of business. He gave me the name of a fleet client he was representing. I had never worked with the company, but also, something made me skeptical about his proposition.

My spirit looked beyond his face, and inwardly I knew I did not want to do business with him. I wasn't sure what the unknown factor was—other than it wasn't money—but I didn't have a good sense about what the man was proposing.

Shortly thereafter, I learned the man went out of business and moved from the area. If I had not heeded the law of discernment, I would have incurred a serious loss.

I do not always heed the law of discernment as I should. Through the years, I have honed my ability to discern. I try to act quickly upon what I sense is best. The times I have made important decisions without adequate deliberation have become reminders to follow the discernment God offers.

Discernment takes two forms: natural and supernatural. Natural discernment comes from intuition. Supernatural discernment is a revelatory gift in which God communicates through our spirit to guide us in perceiving the intents of persons within specific contexts. Both natural and supernatural discernment are essential to wise living and leading.

Fools charge ahead in life without proper guidance and preparation. Yes, I have been a fool at times. Haven't we all? But this gives reason for our reading, "The prudent man looketh well to his going." The law of discernment reminds us of the gift God gives to help us make wise decisions that inevitably influence our lives. And lest we become discouraged, discernment develops through diligence over time.

Prayer

Heavenly Father,

I ask You for spiritual discernment to know and to do Your will. I ask for discernment to know myself and to perceive others. Help me apply the law of discernment to recognize between right and wrong, and to know good, better, and best in others, as well as in myself.

Notes

_____

_____

_____

_____

_____

_____

_____

_____

Discernment is the ability to determine the difference between the good, the bad, and the irrelevant.

—David R. Lockwood

15

Law of Wise Counsel

Read Proverbs 15. Reflect on verse 22.

> Without counsel purposes are disappointed:
> but in the multitude of counselors they are
> established.

Successful business start-ups write business plans based on information received through advisors and industry benchmarks. Whether considering a broad or narrow populace, feasibility studies are conducted to determine market demand and supply, as well as the probability of successfully positioning at a specific locality. If viable, the company researches local market demographics or hires an outside firm to create a marketing plan. When constructing buildings, commercial or residential, input is considered from assessors, engineers, architects, financiers, attorneys, environmental agents, contractors, and neighbors. The law of wise counsel is applied.

The law of wise counsel is not restricted to start-ups or the finances of business. Couples considering marriage are advised to seek wise counsel from pastors, priests, or laypersons. Parents nurturing children are encouraged to acquire wise counsel from extended family members, close friends, or counselors trained to help. Members of most professional organizations have coaches or mentors from whom they may receive wise counsel. Whether we are titans of industry, agents of ministry, or are simply striving for personal growth, we should not lean solely on ourselves to make decisions. We need input from wise counsel.

I am not saying it is wrong to trust our instincts, but I do believe we are remiss to make choices without considering counsel. I have done both, and from my experiences, stepping out on instinct without applying the law of wise counsel has mostly proved unfruitful.

Acquiring broader perspectives is wiser than relying simply on the limits of an individual viewpoint. Obtaining wise counsel offers options that purport successful outcomes. And needless to say, choices determine our health, wealth, and happiness.

The best counselor of all is the Holy Spirit. He is a teacher and an invaluable coach and life partner, and because He is God (and God is omniscient), He knows our future. He can lead us forward.[1]

God wants us to apply the law of wise counsel. When we do, we can expect to experience the rewards of fulfillment.

Prayer

Heavenly Father,

Thank You for giving me Your Holy Spirit as my ultimate Counselor. Help me surround myself with people wiser than I, to learn from them, and to make wise choices. Help me apply the law of wise counsel each day in my life.

Notes

_____

_____

_____

_____

_____

_____

_____

_____

The company we keep is often the counsel we follow.

—David R. Lockwood

16

Law of Divine Guidance

Read Proverbs 16. Reflect on verse 9.

> A man's heart deviseth his way: but the Lord
> directeth his steps.

Taking sure steps and seeing progress in life requires trusting God to guide our steps. God wants us to succeed. More than once He reminds us, "The steps of a good man are ordered by the Lord: and he delighteth in his way. Though he fall, he shall not be utterly cast down: for the Lord upholdeth him with his hand."[1]

God coaches, directs, and leads us. He provides strategies to help us succeed. "Commit thy works unto the Lord, and thy thoughts shall be established."[2] Our thoughts relate to our work, commitments, goals, and achievement.

Even good people make mistakes in judgment. St. Paul tells us we can trust God to not let us fall into circumstances beyond what we can bear.[3] Even though we may stumble, God holds us up. "The law of his God is in his heart; none of his steps shall slide."[4]

The law of divine guidance is God leading us by His Word, His provision, and the voice of His Holy Spirit. God gives us ideas, concepts, contacts, and open doors.

I clearly remember God asking me to dedicate myself to full-time ministry at the age of eighteen. He directed me to open my own business when I was twenty-three. He confirmed to me at the age of twenty-seven that I would be involved in politics, and I have been. When God speaks to me, I write down what He says. My heart is continually on alert and ready to receive divine guidance.

I know and confirm the divine guidance that I receive in my heart by validating what I sense to what the Scriptures say. The guidance we receive from God never contradicts His written Word. Even if I don't hear a direct word in my heart, I trust the Scriptures to give me instruction, direction, and confirmation.

God provides confirmation of His guidance through people, environments, and events. Though it has not happened often, I have experienced times when I knew God was using a person or situation to speak to me. In that moment, the event was a conduit for God's message and direction to me. I have come to understand that God is God, and He can speak through whomever or whatever He chooses.

Pursuing the mission God has for each of us requires applying the law of divine guidance. With the hand of God directing our investments of time and resources, we can believe to experience success in every effort.

Prayer

Heavenly Father,

Help me trust Your divine guidance. Regarding specific plans and goals, help me strategize wisely and work diligently. Help me obey Your direction and guidance. I place my life in Your hands.

Notes

_____

_____

_____

_____

_____

_____

_____

_____

Life's course is too complex to traverse without a GPS: God's Positioning System.

—David R. Lockwood

17

Law of Excellence

Read Proverbs 17. Reflect on verse 27.

> He that hath knowledge spareth his words:
> and a man of understanding is of an excellent
> spirit.

Growing up as an aspiring piano player and singer, I did not produce quality music in the beginning years. I practiced, and I practiced some more. I purposed to produce the best music possible. I pushed myself to apply knowledge and resources during each phase of my musical development. Some call it ambition. For me it was the desire to develop the gifts God had given me.

Sometimes others see talents within us before we recognize them ourselves. Through the help and encouragement of others, we commit to pursue our passions. This is what I did, and as I did, I came upon enviable opportunities and resources, which have allowed me to travel and perform internationally. My only credit is that my effort to excel has offered God something to work with.

Events I have observed have caused me to believe that excellence and mediocrity oppose each other. Average performance warrants stagnation, even termination, but excellence summons promotion. Daniel is an example. His persona resonated excellence. History records that "Daniel was preferred above the presidents and princes, because an excellent spirit was in him; and the king thought to set him over the whole realm."[1]

Daniel was a Jew who was devoted to the only monotheistic religion in the known world at the time, and that caused challenges. He was taken captive into a pagan empire. Of course, he was not the only one, but sometimes company in difficult circumstances amplifies the suffering.

Daniel recognized his giftings and focused on excelling. He applied the law of excellence. Without compromising his principles, he was promoted and stayed in a high position of influence through three transitions of royal power. His life testifies of a God who enabled Daniel to perform every task to the highest standard. Government officials may not have liked his faith, but they could not deny his results.

Daniel applied the law of excellence of which St. Paul speaks: "And whatsoever ye do, do it heartily, as to the Lord, and not unto men; Knowing that of the Lord ye shall receive the reward of the inheritance: for ye serve the Lord Christ."[2]

Let us continue to apply the law of excellence in our talents, work, and legacy. Anything less dishonors an excellent God.

Prayer

Heavenly Father,

Help me to apply the law of excellence to my giftings, my profession, my calling, and my faith. Help me to do everything as unto You. I want to serve You. From You I receive my reward.

Notes

_____

_____

_____

_____

_____

_____

_____

_____

Excellence is the highest state of quality attainable within our collective means and resources.

—David R. Lockwood

18

Law of Wanting It More

Read Proverbs 18. Reflect on verse 1.

> Through desire a man, having separated himself, seeketh and intermeddleth with all wisdom.

I'll never forget the moment I recognized the law of wanting it more. I was service writing for an automotive shop I had recently opened, and I had just closed the sale on a set of tires with a new customer. We exchanged pleasantries and set up a time for the installation. Just as he reached the door on his way out, he turned to me and said, "I like you guys. You seem to want the business more than the competition." He was right.

I had wanted the sale more than I wanted him to walk out without buying tires. It was then that I discovered a principle: I needed to have an earnest intent and to be resolute. That morning I had researched online for prices, then I offered the man the best service package. I had determined that it wasn't just about tires or making a profit (although that is required to stay in business); it was about meeting the needs for which he had come, all the while providing value to our exchange.

Many people give up too soon. When options one and two have been exhausted, they themselves are exhausted. They never make it to options nine or ten. Not Thomas Edison. His famous quest for the filament material of the incandescent lightbulb is an example. He burned through more than one thousand options before finding the correct element. He wanted a solution more than he wanted to quit, and from wanting the solution more, he changed the world.

A difference between mediocre businesspeople and those who are successful is that the latter apply the law of wanting it more. They want it enough to do what it takes. Successful people attempt the necessary number of strategies and pass through failure and disappointment until they reach their goals. Marriages succeed because both partners take the time and effort. They begin with a desire and make it work. Likewise, successful athletes begin with earnest desire and take the time to train to accomplish their goals. Never have we seen an Olympic gold medalist who lacked desire, who didn't want it more.

That morning, I took time with the customer to find the tires he needed. The reward of applying the law of wanting it more is that we SEE | BE | DO | MORE, and develop the resolve to earn a rich reward.

Prayer

Heavenly Father,

Help me to define what I want in life based on the desires You have placed within me. Help me apply the law of wanting it more. Help me to allot the time and resources needed to experience the rewards of wanting it more.

Notes

_____

_____

_____

_____

_____

_____

_____

_____

How badly we want something determines the price we will pay to acquire it.

—David R. Lockwood

19

Law of Rapid Reproof

Read Proverbs 19. Reflect on verse 18.

> Chasten thy son while there is hope, and let not
> thy soul spare for his crying.

We must confront obstacles and issues with wisdom, prudence, tact, and love. Ignoring problems doesn't fade them away. Confrontation most times is painful, and the consequences of not confronting can be worse.

Most of us have observed associates or employees who are asked to do things and refuse. They continue underperforming without regard to suggestions or requests from management or superiors. On several occasions, I have had to make difficult choices. As a business owner, I have never found it easy to correct employees or let them go.

The law of rapid reproof is wisdom that reminds me to not put off confronting. It prompts me to communicate with a manager, employee, or vendor. When problems arise, I have found it best to offer options. The individual can elect to change or choose not to remain with the organization I lead.

The confrontation awakens the person to realize the gravity of the problem and the need for resolution.

I seldom want to be hard or difficult. I always want to be fair and honest, known as a person of integrity who does what he says he will do. Too often we live or work with individuals who voice a rule but do not follow through. When this happens, credibility is injured, if not destroyed.

Security in one's identity is required to withstand scrutiny and correction. Wise people are grateful for the opportunity to change. They know it promotes personal and professional growth.

The story of Eli and his two wicked sons, Hophni and Phinehas, illustrates the results of not living by the law of rapid reproof. Both Hophni and Phinehas committed sacrilegious atrocities within and outside the temple. Eli failed to discipline and correct his sons, and instead made excuses for them. For this reason, God excommunicated Eli's family from the priesthood. Eli and his two sons died on the same fateful day.[1]

Some people diminish their personal power by creating excuses for not confronting. Weakness in adversity is not a winning strategy. As leaders, we are responsible to set the tone of environment and apply the law of rapid reproof.

Prayer

Heavenly Father,

Let nothing negative grow in my mind, heart, environment, or relationships. Help me be quick to correct and reprove, and quick to love and appreciate. I want to apply the law of rapid reproof.

Notes

_____

_____

_____

_____

_____

_____

_____

_____

Life is meant to be challenging and difficult at times, in order to prove what we are capable of overcoming.

—David R. Lockwood

20

Law of Mercy

Read Proverbs 20. Reflect on verse 28.

> Mercy and truth preserve the king: and his
> throne is upheld by mercy.

The law of mercy is most welcomed following the previous law of rapid reproof. Jesus tells us that those who give mercy are blessed. Those who give mercy receive mercy.[1] In business, as in relationships, mercy extends beyond what would be viewed as fair. One can act equitably, apply justice, and withhold mercy by not providing a second chance.

When we apply the law of mercy, we act in love from the perspective that we believe the individual can and will change. In my business, more than once I have had to let an employee go because I no longer had the confidence that the person could or would change. But on occasion, a mistake has been made and, although it angered me to the point of wanting to let the person go, I knew the law of mercy was what needed to be applied.

None of us is perfect. Each of us has days when efforts, influences, or outcomes are not favorable. On these days, we need to remember the principle Jesus taught: "Do unto others as we would want them to do unto us."[2]

I spoke with a friend a few weeks ago, and we reminisced about a season when I led the music department for a local congregation in my early twenties. He and several others played instruments and sang, and I led the band. I had—and still have—much to learn as a leader. As we conversed over dinner, I recalled that I had been impatient, intolerant, poorly organized, and not all that talented; but they put up with me nonetheless. I mentioned to him, "The ignorant way I acted toward you all, it's a wonder we're still friends today."

"Your methods were a little unconventional," he told me. "But we liked you, and we saw past your faults." Mercy requires that kind of long-range vision.

Jesus tells of a king who applied the law of mercy by forgiving his servant an astronomical debt that would have been impossible to repay. The forgiven servant, however, had the person who owed *him* money thrown in jail. After hearing of this atrocity, the king repealed the law of mercy and had the first servant thrown in jail for life.[3] The law of rapid reproof was applied. The king knew when to show mercy and when not to.

May we each be as wise as this king. And may we appreciate the people who see past our faults and practice the law of mercy.

Prayer

Heavenly Father,

Help me apply the law of mercy. Help me be wise. Holy Spirit, I ask You for discernment to know how to best demonstrate mercy. I want to be a person who walks in love toward others.

Notes

_____

_____

_____

_____

_____

_____

_____

_____

Mercy is like a bank account. We can only draw from what we have previously deposited.
—David R. Lockwood

21

Law of Diligence

Read Proverbs 21. Meditate on verse 5.

> The thoughts of the diligent tend only to plenteousness; but of every one that is hasty only to want.

Most of us have met at least one person who one day appears to be set on conquering the world, and the next day is deflated, unmotivated, and burned out. Most of us probably just shake our heads, hoping silently we are not the next to be like them.

Success is found in daily habits. Consistency is crucial. Diligence is repetition that requires assuming continual responsibility. It can mean doing the right thing over and over again, often to the point of boredom.

Right habits are seldom emotionally exciting. Rare is the day when I feel a thrill of ecstasy stepping onto the treadmill. I do feel better getting onto the weigh scales afterward. Often it's not the development of good habits that we enjoy, but the results that those habits bring.

Here are three verses from Proverbs regarding diligence:

> He becometh poor that dealeth with a slack
> hand: but the hand of the diligent maketh rich.[1]
> The hand of the diligent will rule, while the
> slothful will be put to forced labor.[2]
> Seest thou a man diligent in his business? He
> shall stand before kings; he shall not stand
> before mean men.[3]

Occasionally we observe commercials for music concerts offering VIP, backstage, all-access passes to meet the stars. We see VIP hotel offers with concierge and private luxury entertainment packages. It would appear that many people want to buy their way to greatness, but experience reveals that right daily habits are what award us greatness. Many want to be persons of wealth and influence; few are willing to pay the price.

Patience is another aspect of diligence. As mentioned, to haste to riches is not advised. Working consistently on a routine basis is a better strategy. *Anything worth doing is worth doing daily* is the refrain we should consider.

One way to apply the law of diligence is to daily read God's Word, listen to His direction, and pursue our dreams. Then, as a winner crossing the finish line, we will finish our mission with distinction and honor. We will receive the reward of having accomplished the destiny God created us for.

Prayer

Heavenly Father,

I ask You for the grace and discipline to apply the law of diligence. Daily help me to be consistent, patient, thorough, and perseverant in the pursuit of my goals. Help me to keep myself motivated, and to trust You for the best possible outcome.

Notes

_____

_____

_____

_____

_____

_____

_____

_____

If I had to choose, I would take discipline with
persistence over talent without character any day.
—David R. Lockwood

22

Law of a Good Name

Read Proverbs 22. Reflect on verse 1.

> A good name is rather to be chosen than great
> riches, and loving favor rather than silver and
> gold.

My first successful business startup began with a one-page lease and a five-minute phone conversation that landed me a ten-thousand-dollar loan. First Class Auto began with nothing more than my word. To my creditors, I promised to pay on time. To my customers, I promised to pursue excellence in service. Thanks to much hard work and God's grace, my team and I have been able to keep both promises.

As a consumer, you have probably noticed that most prospective clients prefer firms with good reputations. Our company strives to give customers confidence. We reinforce the fact that we possess the skills to do the job. More importantly, we demonstrate that we possess the character to be trusted.

In every business transaction, we purpose to look people in the eyes, shake their hands when appropriate, give our word, and let them know that we are committed to completing the task with excellence on time. I communicate and follow up as necessary. Trust is the result of confidence fulfilled. Respect is the reputation that one develops through building and maintaining trust.

Vendors want to know that a company will pay its bills on time. Children want to know that their parents will be consistent in love and discipline. Creditors want to know that a borrower will repay a loan. Applying the law of a good name means we strive to have a positive and consistent reputation.

Building a good name develops in part through confidence in our God-given ability. On rare occasion, I have committed my company to a task that I was unsure how we would accomplish. However, I have known who to reach out to, whose advise to follow, and what resources to assemble to fulfill my commitment. I have learned, as have others, that I don't have to be an expert at everything. What I don't know, I can find out. But I do have to follow through.

The law of a good name exhorts us to foster confidence, trust, and respect. It resonates the significance of keeping our word. It reminds us to do our best, because at the end of the day, our true asset is a good name that others can trust. With God, we also trust and respect Him because His name is good.

Prayer

Heavenly Father,

Help me to develop a consistent, dependable, and positive reputation. Help me be a person of integrity and accountability. I want to establish a name that glorifies You—one that people can trust. Help me apply the law of a good name.

Notes

_____

_____

_____

_____

_____

_____

_____

_____

My name is all I have. It is all God has, and it appears to be working well for Him!
                                                —David R. Lockwood

23

Law of Hope

Read Proverbs 23. Reflect on verses 17–18.

> Let not thine heart envy sinners: but be thou in
> the fear of the Lord all the day long. For surely
> there is an end; and thine expectation shall not
> be cut off.

Hope is a flame kindled by faith, sparked by love. All three virtues are decisions and actions, not mere feelings.

In the proverb, when we consider that our expectation will not be cut off, we are assured that the Source of our hope will never fail. Scripture tells us that God knew what He was doing when He made us, and that His intents for us are good, filled with peace and hope.[1] God didn't plan our lives with evil in mind. He thinks about us, cares for us, and wants us to succeed. It is in His plan that we have hope.

When we couple our hope with the faith that St. Paul describes, we realize that what we envision in our heart is not always what we see with our physical eyes.[2] When we apply the law of hope, faith depicts what is the spiritual reality of our goals on the inside until they come to exist physically on the outside. It is with hope that we are able to trust.

When we discover that God has a plan for us, we can cooperate with the Holy Spirit to see its design and purpose completed. We aren't able to see the end from the beginning as He does. We don't immediately perceive all the details relevant to our calling. We do, however, apply the law of hope for God's plan to be fulfilled.

In my journey, I have learned to live in the moment, to do what I know to do, and to trust that further instructions will be revealed as I progress. I love God, which is why I choose to obey. I act in faith for the present. I carry hope for the future. I exercise faith for what I can control. I possess hope for the elements of life that are beyond my control.

Let's say that in my life's journey I am at A, and I want to get to Z. I know steps B and C, but I don't know steps Q through U. I haven't yet discovered them. I can't dwell on Q through U. What I can do is act and focus on B and C, trusting that when I complete those steps, D and E will be revealed, and so forth, until I get to Z.

Love gives us motivation to act. Faith makes us productive and expectant in the present. Hope keeps our eyes looking forward toward our destiny. When we apply the law of hope, we are encouraged to love and have faith in God and His plan for our lives.

Prayer

Heavenly Father,

I place my trust in Your plan, purpose, and destiny for my life. Help me to continually apply the law of hope, exercise my faith, act in love, and take steps to accomplish my purpose. I know that as I am faithful where I am, You will reveal my future.

Notes

_____

_____

_____

_____

_____

_____

_____

_____

Faith stands on love's shoulders to reach for a hope-cast horizon. God honors the reaching.
—David R. Lockwood

24

Law of Getting Back Up

Read Proverbs 24. Reflect on verse 16.

> For a just man falleth seven times, and riseth up
> again: but the wicked shall fall into mischief.

I am inspired each time I read this verse, specifically when I see the number of times the just man falls. The number seven signifies completion and wholeness. While falling may not be a popular subject, failure is a great teacher in conducting us toward success. The key is in renaming the moment.

When failure occurs, a proper response is to name the lesson learned, apply the lesson toward improvements, and make changes that will lead toward better results. The just man in the passage falls seven times, the number of times necessary in order to eventually succeed.

Are we willing to fail to succeed? The first business I attempted failed miserably. I lost everything and lived in my car for several months while I restabilized. I learned lessons, lost the fear of losing everything, and went at it again. My second business performed much better; however, several years into it, I made a couple of bad financial decisions that almost cost me the business. I had vendor bills piling up, and employees counting on me. I cried to God in prayer, and I'll never forget His simple, reassuring response: "Keep walking." I obeyed, made changes, and we have grown more prosperous every year since.

Failure becomes definitive when we stop making progress, when we decide not to keep walking, when we shift our effort and motivation into park. We go *through* failure, not stay in it. St. Paul assures us that God provides a way out of every trying circumstance we may face.[1] The key is learning the way out, making corrections to our methods, and moving on.

We all make mistakes. Persisting in error leads to destruction. Humbling ourselves to recognize faults, make adjustments, and move forward brings success.

The law of getting back up also applies to relationships. How many times has someone broken their promise to us? How often have we broken our promises? We don't like to admit it, but it happens, and when it does, trust is broken or injured.

We are human. As humans, we must have the will to get back up, to forgive, and to keep our sight on the good. The law of getting back up means we do not quit.

Prayer

Heavenly Father,

Help me to learn from failure, rename the moment, get back up, and persist. Help me to follow the dreams You have placed within me. I believe that from every failure, I will apply the law of getting back up. I riseth up again, and believe Your mercy and grace see me through.

Notes

_____

_____

_____

_____

_____

_____

_____

_____

We are never failures if we keep getting back up.
—David R. Lockwood

25

Law of Due Process

Read Proverbs 25. Reflect on verse 4.

> Take away the dross from the silver, and there
> shall come forth a vessel for the finer.

God uses process. Some people may like to imagine that God takes His scepter and in an instant enacts change, but from what I have experienced and observed, most times God uses spiritual, intellectual, emotional, physical, relational, professional, and financial processes to bring about change. The processes God uses grow us up. And though we might not like to acknowledge it, what takes place during the process can be as or more important than the original intended outcome.

I enjoy taking road trips. I like focusing on the destination. My mind arrives before I do. When I play Monopoly I want to draw the card, *Collect $200 GO*—none of this continual rolling of dice to get to where I want to land. Fortunately, God does not use casting lots to guide our steps. He does, however, expect us to take them, one at a time.

Process supersedes destination. Even though it is important to maintain focus and to pursue clear goals and directives for our lives, only God sees the fullness of the future He desires for us. Thank goodness God has more than one route to direct us to our destination.

I have on occasion questioned past decisions I have made, personal and business, wondering how my life would have been had I made different choices. Every time I pause to consider these possibilities, the Lord reminds me that one way or another, because I belong to Him, I will end up where I need to be. The law of due process facilitates the principle: *It's not how you start, but how you finish.*

At times we may ask, What about our freedom of will? We are free to choose.[1] God gives us that option, but assuming we choose life and success, then we understand that a man's heart devises his way, but God directs his steps.[2] Our responsibilities as humans reside within our control, but our destinies as eternal beings reside within the power of His grace. God is greater than our heart.

When we are faced with adversity, or when we are challenged to grow beyond our comfort, let us embrace God's process of maturity for our lives. Even when we cannot clearly see the expected destination, we can trust that God's will is "good, and acceptable, and perfect."[3] If we allow the law of due process to work in our lives, we will arrive where we need to be, and more likely enjoy the journey.

Prayer

Heavenly Father,

I trust Your processes. Thank You for developing within me the traits and qualities that will cause me to arrive at my destination. Help me appreciate and apply the law of due process.

Notes

_____

_____

_____

_____

_____

_____

_____

_____

God is just as interested in our process of internal development as He is in our arrival at external achievement.

—David R. Lockwood

26

Law of Loyalty

Read Proverbs 26. Reflect on verse 20.

> Where no wood is, there the fire goeth out: so
> where there is no talebarer, the strife ceaseth.

I once left a company over a disagreement in policy. Others had left over similar concerns and had gossiped about existing leadership. I chose not to. I recalled the verse, "A faithful man shall abound with blessings."[1] I decided to protect the owners and their reputation.

What the company did was not morally wrong. It was simply something I disagreed with on personal principle. Through the years, I have maintained a good relationship with the owners, and have been asked on several occasions to provide services for their corporation, which became opportunities that never would have opened for me had I not remained loyal to character, or if I had burned bridges as I left.

We never know when we will need to draw from a relationship we have built in the past. If we have nurtured trust and respect, and have defended the honor and reputation of friends and colleagues, in the future we can benefit from having applied the law of loyalty. Andy Stanley says it like this: "Loyalty publicly results in leverage privately."[2]

The objective is not to pursue leverage from others, but it can happen as a result. Too many people are quick to ostracize associates or acquaintances when personally or professionally convenient. We must remember that no one is perfect. If others make mistakes, we inevitably will make them too. If we sow loyalty in protecting others, we will reap loyalty and mercy in return.[3] God will repay.[4]

I am not saying we shouldn't confront moral or ethical failings in our relationships. The purpose of loyalty is not to conceal sins that perpetuate wrong behavior. However, we can choose not to dishonor or humiliate people when they are less than their best. Instead of perpetuating negative comments—whether true or false—we can look for the good and comment on these. We can spotlight our attention on what is done right and not broadcast the noticeable wrongs.

Edifying the reputations of others often opens doors of opportunity for us. Being positive and applying the law of loyalty causes our own careers and aspirations to rise. No one arrives alone.

Prayer

Heavenly Father,

Help me to be loyal to You. Help me live the law of loyalty among family, friends, colleagues, and those whom I serve. Thank You that the opportunities I make happen for others, You make happen for me.

Notes

_____

_____

_____

_____

_____

_____

_____

_____

True loyalty cannot be bought. It is priceless, which is what makes it so valuable.

—David R. Lockwood

27

Law of Daily Evaluation

Read Proverbs 27. Reflect on verse 23.

> Be diligent to know the state of thy flocks, and
> look well to thy herds.

Many people envision themselves doing something other than what they are doing, or being somewhere other than where they are, but they don't know how to get from where they are to where they want to be. Some are even unsure of where they are in regard to their purpose in life.

In business and politics, advisors talk about strategy. One strategy I have used in business is SWOT, which focuses on strengths, weaknesses, opportunities, and threats. When I transfer this paradigm to my faith, it means taking inventory of what I can offer to God for Him to multiply back into my life. As I self-examine, I apply the law of daily evaluation.

Every area of our lives can be viewed as a chart of accounts: our faith and walk with God, our intellectual or emotional well-being, and our physical health. Every relationship in our lives can be viewed as an account, similar to that of a bank.

To see the similarity: we cannot place a demand on an account or an area of our lives that we have not first deposited into. If we do not know the status of our accounts, we will not know if we are in the black or overdrawn. We cannot implement a strategy of reaching our potential with a war chest that is overspent. We will lose. That is why the verse states we should be diligent to know the state of our accounts.[1]

Businesspeople check their bank accounts frequently and routinely. Some check daily to verify cash flow. Family members and people in relationships should do likewise to assess whether they have deposited love, care, affection, and whether they have invested more than what they expect to withdraw or ask of these relationships. If a demand is being placed on our faith, we must ask, "To what extent have I filled my heart with God's Word so I can draw from it during this time?"

I suggest applying the law of daily evaluation to our investments. If it is important, it will be done. If areas of our life need attention—as accounts that need deposits—make investing in these areas a priority. Then when the need comes, we won't find our spirits, families, finances, or futures facing a deficit. We will have been diligent to look well upon that which we hold.

Prayer

Heavenly Father,

Help me diligently evaluate my spiritual, emotional, physical, relational, and financial state, and to supplement and invest in the areas of my life that need care and attention. Thank You for helping me apply the law of daily evaluation.

Notes

_____

_____

_____

_____

_____

_____

_____

_____

Know where you are, or you'll eventually find yourself where you didn't want to be.

—David R. Lockwood

28

Law of Generosity

Read Proverbs 28. Reflect on verse 27.

> He that giveth unto the poor shall not lack: but
> he that hideth his eyes shall have many a curse.

The law of generosity includes sowing seed and giving alms. Here's an example. One of my first financial ventures was a car wash and detailing business. I was not well known in the community, and I didn't have a marketing budget other than a few flyers and word-of-mouth advertising, so I decided to work and give away as many details as I could.

I spent hours and hours washing, waxing, shampooing, Q-tipping air-conditioning vents, and extracting dog hair and debris to establish credibility. I literally gave weeks of my time away. Now years later, the business continues to expand and grow in profits. I attribute its success to sowing generous seed.

Another example of the law of generosity is mirrored in the many letters our team has received from nonprofits and community organizations thanking us for in-kind and monetary contributions to humanitarian causes in the state and beyond. Such charity results in both natural and spiritual benefits. The natural benefits demonstrate commitment to the community and supportive citizenship. They also promote the reputation of the individual and company contributing. Frequently, revenue is generated from referrals as a result of the law of generosity.

The spiritual benefit of applying the law of generosity is observed through giving alms. When we give alms, God promises to repay: "He that hath pity upon the poor lendeth unto the Lord; and that which he hath given will he pay him again."[1] What we lend to the Lord, He gives back. This concept is distinct from sowing seed, which incites a return on investment of thirty-, sixty-, or one hundred-fold.[2] Charity is meeting a requested need. Sowing seed is investing for a desired outcome.

Generosity is one of God's many characteristics, and it is one of the traits our country is known for. America has historically given much to community needs, missions, and outreaches. We must keep in view the value of applying the law of generosity in our personal lives, our businesses, our communities, our country, and our world. When we give, we gain.

Prayer

Heavenly Father,

Thank You for helping me identify good opportunities in which to sow seed. Also, help me be generous in charity and alms to meet critical community needs, providing more than hope for those less fortunate. Make me a person who applies the law of generosity with love, time, and resources.

Notes

_____

_____

_____

_____

_____

_____

_____

_____

God is a giver. People who spend time with Him begin to assume His giving nature.

—David R. Lockwood

29

Law of Clear Vision

Read Proverbs 29. Reflect on verse 18.

> Where there is no vision, the people perish: but
> he that keepeth the law, happy is he.

Vision is a picture of what a person or organization wants to become, perform, and possess. We could say that vision is the potential reality of ourselves in the future. Goals we achieve are steps, benchmarks to measure our progress toward that picture.

Vision exists on two levels: natural and spiritual. Natural vision changes and adapts to circumstances such as markets and economy, relationships and careers. Spiritual vision does not change. Spiritual vision is how God sees us coming to His "expected end."[1] Through our relationship with Jesus Christ, we come to know that expected end.

Both natural vision and spiritual vision must be clear and focused to prompt achievement. "The mind of man plans his way, but the Lord directs his steps."[2] Human vision includes writing out business and marketing plans, family financial plans, career choices, educational pursuits, and seeking networking opportunities. Divine vision becomes clear through dreams, visions, miraculous interventions, words of prophesy, and *rhema*, or inspired words we sense God revealing to us through His Word and Holy Spirit. The law of clear vision represents the alignment of both spiritual and natural vision.

I think back to when I started one of my businesses. I possessed spiritual vision, but I failed to articulate adequate natural vision. I planned survival tactics on a daily and sometimes hourly basis. Looking back, God saw it all, including the intent of my heart. However, if I had cleared the fog from my natural vision by writing adequate strategies and procedures, days would have been filled with greater clarity and assurance of how I would successfully serve God through the endeavor of running a business.

We know it is easier to see from past to present than from present to future. For this reason, we must apply the law of clear vision. Now and then we may need to defog the clouds of distractions and fears that hinder our visibility. Ultimately, however, we trust God to provide His vision for our lives and submit our human vision and planning to His. We trust that our decisions honor God, and that He causes our steps to lead us in the direction of His vision for us.

Prayer

Heavenly Father,

I ask for wisdom to apply the law of clear vision so that I may align my human vision to Your divine vision for me. Help me keep Your laws. Blind my view of distractions and fears. In You I trust.

Notes

_____

_____

_____

_____

_____

_____

_____

_____

Vision is captured in the heart. When the heart sets the destination, the mind lays the strategy to achieve.

—David R. Lockwood

30

Law of Honor

Read Proverbs 30. Reflect on verses 12–13.

> There is a generation that is pure in their
> own eyes, and yet is not washed from their
> filthiness. There is a generation, O how lofty
> are their eyes! And their eyelids are lifted up.

Mankind is created in the image of God.[1] When we honor other people, we honor their divine qualities.[2] We speak to their hearts.

Honor appears to be waning in our society. A self-centeredness has surfaced in our generation that fails to recognize the investments and sacrifices of previous generations. Deserving individuals often are not appreciated or respected as they should be.

Honor for me began in my family. My parents taught me at a young age to honor them.[3] They also taught me to respect others in authority. Growing up away from extended family frequently offered opportunities for me to honor friends and associates of my parents. I developed a respect for the many adults I grew up with who were committed to giving their lives to a mission larger than themselves.

Honor does four things for us, particularly when we are growing and committed to excellence. First, honor toward God and others brings divine blessings on our relationships.[4] Second, honoring others distinguishes us from those who show no honor. Demonstrating and communicating honor has given me an effective and competitive edge. I do not mean superficial platitudes—I mean profound, genuine, and sincere respect.

Third, honor edifies and makes those we honor feel valued. It reminds them of their sense of worth, which is a reminder everyone needs and appreciates. And fourth, honor opens doors to relationships and divine contacts. Honor has given me the opportunity to meet with highly successful people, and has granted me access that has amplified my insight and accelerated my business and life education.

Through practice and experience, I have learned that honor is demonstrated in protocol and demeanor, in communication and demonstration of respect, and in deference to a person's knowledge, experience, and results. Honor is also exhibited in financial contributions. When I chose to gift monies or to do business with a person, I honor them.

Honor is a divine quality. When we honor others, we recognize the divine within them.

Prayer

Heavenly Father,

Help me honor You in my thoughts, words, and actions. Help me apply the law of honor to my parents, persons in authority, family, friends, and associates. I want my life to honor You.

Notes

_____

_____

_____

_____

_____

_____

_____

_____

Tragedy occurs when we possess genius and not honor.

—David R. Lockwood

31

Law of Greatness

Read Proverbs 31. Reflect on verses 8–9.

> Open thy mouth for the dumb in the cause of
> all such as are appointed to destruction. Open
> thy mouth, judge righteously, and plead the
> cause of the poor and needy.

Words are uttered. Actions are heard. Jesus knew this. He taught that anyone who wants to be great must be a servant of others.[1]

I like to view service as three things. First, as an occupation or function, service is action. Second, service is helping. I prefer to regard service as solving problems. Third, service is contributing to the welfare of others. It is an outward focus, not an inner, self-directed focus. In sum, service is action that solves problems for and adds value to others. Service comes from within and is demonstrated without.

When we read about men and women who have become esteemed as heroes, we come to understand that greatness is achieved through service. Great people become great because they solve great problems.

When I started one of my businesses in Colorado, I had several goals I wanted to meet. I wanted to make an equitable living, and I wanted to develop a business that solved a basic problem or need for people. One need people have is transportation. In the United States, most people want to drive their own car. Servicing cars seemed to be an option.

As a businessman in the community, it was not long before I saw opportunities beyond servicing cars. Town council had vacancies. The Chamber of Commerce needed board members. Community sporting leagues and humanitarian organizations needed volunteers and financial support. It seemed that requests to serve continually welcomed me.

I could have rescinded my time and convinced others and myself that I had nothing to share, but that is not what we practiced growing up. Saturdays my father would take my brother and me to *comedores* (similar to soup kitchens). We served breakfast to children and their mothers instead of watching Saturday morning cartoons. Through these experiences and others, I learned that the value and reward of service extends far beyond gains received when focusing on self-centered interests.

I would have been wiser if I had applied *Business Laws from Proverbs* when I first started in business, but through my ventures I have learned. My hope is that we each come to experience the law of greatness by climbing the rungs of service.

Prayer

Heavenly Father,

Help me apply Your law of greatness without regard to class or race. I want to share the resources You have given me with members of my family, community, and beyond. Help me serve as Jesus did.

Notes

_____

_____

_____

_____

_____

_____

_____

_____

Greatness is found in the magnitude of service toward others, not in the loftiness of personal ambition.

—David R. Lockwood

Notes

Law of Association
    1 John 16:13

Law of Seeking and Finding
    1 Proverbs 2:7
    2 Proverbs 2:8
    3 Proverbs 2:9
    4 Proverbs 2:11

Law of Growing
    1 Matthew 7:19
    2 John Maxwell team; August 8, 2014; Orlando, Florida.

Law of Access
    1 Genesis 39
    2 Matthew 7:6

Law of Action
    1 James 2:20
    2 Deuteronomy 28:12

Law of Focus
    1 Proverbs 7:9
    2 Romans 8:28

Law of Creating Favor
    1 Proverbs 3:14
    2 Proverbs 8:11

Law of Preparation
    1 Matthew 6:11

Law of the Blessing
    1 Isaiah 1:19
    2 Deuteronomy 28:1–14
    3 Psalm 3:8

Law of Spreading Good News
    1 Romans 10:14
    2 Proverbs 11:31
    3 Psalm 27:13

Law of Right Speaking
 1 James 3:8

Law of Wise Counsel
 1 John 14:26

Law of Divine Guidance
 1 Psalms 37:23–24
 2 Proverbs 16:3
 3 1 Corinthians 10:13
 4 Psalm 37:31

Law of Excellence
 1 Daniel 6:3
 2 Colossians 3:23

Law of Rapid Reproof
 1 1 Samuel 4:11

Law of Mercy
 1 Matthew 5:7
 2 Matthew 7:12
 3 Matthew 18:23–34

Law of Diligence
 1 Proverbs 10:4
 2 Proverbs 12:24
 3 Proverbs 22:29

Law of Hope
 1 Jeremiah 29:11
 2 Hebrew 11:1
 3 James 2:26
 4 Hebrew 11:1

Law of Getting Back Up
 1 1 Corinthians 10:13

Law of Due Process
 1 Deuteronomy 30:19
 2 Proverbs 16:9
 3 Romans 12:2

Law of Loyalty
 1 Proverbs 28:20
 2 A. Stanley and L. Jones, *Communicating for Change: Seven Keys to Irresistible Communication* (Colorado Springs, Colorado: Multnomah Books, 2006).
 3 Matthew 7:2
 4 Romans 12:19

Law of Daily Evaluation
 1 Proverbs 27:23

Law of Generosity
    1 Proverbs 19:17
    2 Matthew 13:8

Law of Clear Vision
    1 Jeremiah 29:11
    2 Proverbs 16:9

Law of Honor
    1 Genesis 1:27
    2 1 Peter 2:17
    3 Ephesians 6:2
    4 Psalm 84:11

Law of Greatness
    1 Matthew 20:26

DAVIDRICHARD

SEE | BE | DO | MORE

To book David to speak at your organization, or for additional information and resources, call 866-317-9251.

David Lockwood
PO Box 2494
Granby, CO 80446
davidrlockwood.com

Printed in the United States
By Bookmasters